Revolution and Romanticism, 1789-1834
A series of facsimile reprints chosen and introduced by
Jonathan Wordsworth
University Lecturer in Romantic Studies at Oxford

Mant
The simpliciad 1808

Richard Mant

The simpliciad
1808

Woodstock Books
Oxford and New York
1991

This edition first published 1991 by
Woodstock Books
Spelsbury House, Spelsbury, Oxford OX7 3JR
and
Woodstock Books
Wordsworth Trust America
Department of English, City College
Convent Ave and 138th St, New York, N.Y. 10031

New matter copyright © Woodstock Books 1991
Reproduced by permission from a copy in the
Bodleian Library, Oxford, Shelfmark 280 f. 2304 (1)

British Library Cataloguing in Publication Data
Mant, Richard, b. 1776
  The simpliciad 1808. – (Revolution and romanticism, 1789-1834)
  I. Title II. Series
  821.7
  ISBN 1854770764

Printed and bound in Great Britain by
Smith Settle
Otley, West Yorkshire LS21 3JP

Introduction

The Reverend William Mant, anonymous author of the *Simpliciad* (1808), was not given to self-doubt. *Lyrical ballads* had gone through four editions, 1798-1805, winning (sometimes grumpy) praise from a wide variety of critics, but he was not a man to take note of changing attitudes, changing poetic decorum. Mant is the conservative reader of his day, well informed, not untalented, no more prejudiced than most. To read him is to understand the weariness in Wordsworth's voice as he speaks of a great poet having to create the taste by which he is enjoyed. In 1806 Mant had published a volume of somewhat innocuous poems himself. The *Simpliciad* was prompted by honest indignation on the appearance of Wordsworth's *Poems in two volumes* the following year. Such triviality could not go unpunished! With Jeffrey's 1802 review of *Thalaba* in mind, Mant purports to attack the Lakers in general:

> Poets, who fix their visionary sight
> On Sparrow's eggs in prospect of delight,
> With fervent welcome greet the glow-worm's flame,
> Put it to bed and bless it by its name;
> Hunt waterfalls, that gallop down the hills:
> And dance with dancing laughing daffodils;
> Or measure ponds from side to side,
> And find them three feet long and two feet wide:
> Poets, with brother donkey in the dell
> Of mild equality who fain would dwell;
> With brother lark or brother robin fly,
> Or flutter with half-brother butterfly. . . .

Nine Wordsworth poems are mocked in succession, with an intermission for Coleridge's political allegory, *Address to a young ass*. In each case Mant has quoted in his footnote the passage that gives him 'authority'. 'The school is incapable of caricature', he comments in the Dedication, 'if a smile be raised by my illustrations, it will be heightened by a perusal of the originals whence they are drawn.' Times have changed. It comes as a shock to find under the heading of the evidently ridiculous:

And dance with dancing laughing daffodills, &c.
  I wander'd lonely as a cloud
  That floats on high o'er vales and hills,
  When all at once I saw a crowd,
  A host of *dancing daffodills*.

  * * *

  A Poet could not but be gay
  In such a *laughing* company.

  * * *

  And then my heart with pleasure fills,
  And *dances with the daffodills*.

Jeffrey had singled out 'an affectation of great simplicity and familiarity of language' as the 'most distinguishing symbol' of the Lake School. In his view, the origins of the school lay in a combination of Rousseau's primitivism, 'the simplicity and energy . . . of Kotzebue and Schiller' and the 'homeliness' of Cowper. Cowper was politically neutral, but Rousseau had been among the fathers of the Revolution; Schiller and Kotzebue (represented by *The robbers* and *Lovers' vows*) had put their simplicity and energy to the purpose of undermining social order. With such a pedigree the Lakers' affectation could not be seen as apolitical. Jeffrey was aware of the originality of *Lyrical ballads*, but saw the volume as a 'flagrant act of hostility', a betrayal at once of poetic and social decorum:

The language of the higher and more cultivated orders may fairly be presumed to be better than that of their inferiors. . . . But the mischief of this new system is not confined to the depravation of language only; it extends to the sentiments and emotions, and leads to the debasement of all those feelings which poetry is designed to communicate. . . . Next after great familiarity of language, there is nothing that appears to them so meritorious as perpetual exaggeration of thought.

Mant is less affronted than Jeffrey, less inclined to see things in political terms, but many of his assumptions are the same. The Lakers do not merely let themselves down by their simplicity, they trivialize poetry by making exaggerated claims for commonplace experience. With *Daffodils* we have no doubt that he is wrong, but what of *The sparrow's nest*? Mant's reference to

> Poets, who fix their visionary sight
> On Sparrow's eggs in prospect of delight . . .

is footnoted by lines that carry for most of us a childish sense of wonderment:

> Look, five blue eggs are gleaming there!
> Few *visions* have I seen more fair,
> Nor many *prospects of delight*,
> More pleasing than that simple sight!

Are the italicized words not an 'exaggeration of thought'? If not, what of *The daisy*, introduced by Mant with the uncharitable comment, 'I know not whether a more perfect instance of silliness is to be detected in the whole farrago of the school, than the following stanza':

> Thou wander'st the wide world about,
> Uncheck'd by pride or scrupulous doubt,
> With friends to greet thee, or without,

> Yet pleased and willing;
> Meek, yielding to occasion's call,
> And all things suffering from all,
> THY FUNCTION APOSTOLICAL
>   IN PEACE FULFILLING.

Mant's capitalization forces us either to side with him, or to explain Wordsworth's extraordinary language. Already human to the point of wandering the wide world, meek and suffering, the daisy (etymologically the 'eye of day') is finally a witness, or messenger, of God. As so often with the 1802 lyrics published in *Poems in two volumes*, we are uncertain on what level the claims are being made. Wordsworth's later distinction of imagination and fancy doesn't really help. He has at this period a fanciful imagination. To Mant both his wonderment and his playfulness are silly – 'simple' in the unflattering sense of the word applied to those who are 'not all there'.

The *Simpliciad* is not a subtle or discriminating satire. It has neither the brilliance of the *Anti-Jacobin* parodists (1797-8), nor the intuitive sympathy of Hogg's *Poetic mirror* (1816). The lyrical ballads are condemned without exception. After quoting (in derisive italics) beautiful excerpts from *Resolution and independence*,

> Motionless as a cloud the old man stood,
> That heareth not the loud winds when they call . . .

Mant takes leave of the author, 'with an apology for attempting to give anything like a fair specimen of [his] solemn buffoonery'. Bringing together numinous lines from the *Ode* and *Personal talk*, in a way that nearly approaches genius, he seems unaware that his own verse has been amazingly enhanced:

The cataracts blow their trumpets from the steep,
Awaken'd echoes through the mountains throng,
And kettles whisper their faint undersong.

For Wordsworth simplicity was a stripping away of the inessential. He did not, as Jeffrey assumed (on a rather frontal reading of the Preface), wish either to write in the language of Cumbrian shepherds, or to express the actual pattern of their thoughts. He wished, in his quest for the essential and abiding, to learn from those whose way of life seemed to him 'more sane, pure and permanent'. The tendency to 'exaggerated thought', disliked by Jeffrey and mocked in the *Simpliciad*, was the clearest sign of a new poetic decorum. 'The feeling therein developed', Wordsworth wrote succinctly of the lyrical ballads, 'gives importance to the action and situation, and not the action and situation to the feeling.' It was a reversal of traditional standards that Mant, for one, could not accept. To him a daisy was a daisy. He was a sort of intellectual Peter Bell:

A primrose by a river's brim
A yellow primrose was to him,
   And it was nothing more.

J W

THE SIMPLICIAD;

A SATIRICO-DIDACTIC POEM.

CONTAINING

HINTS FOR THE SCHOLARS OF THE NEW SCHOOL,

Suggested by Horace's Art of Poetry,

AND IMPROVED BY A CONTEMPLATION OF THE WORKS

OF

THE FIRST MASTERS.

Simplex munditiis.—HORACE.
Undeck'd save with herself.—MILTON.

London:

PRINTED FOR JOHN JOSEPH STOCKDALE,
NO. 41, PALL-MALL.

1808.

T. Gillet, Printer, Fleet-street.

TO

Messrs. William Wordsworth,
Robert Southey, and S. T. Coleridge.

GENTLEMEN,

ALLOW me to dedicate to you the following Anthology; for it is in fact little more than a collection of flowers, unless I adopt the language of one of your triumvirate, and call them weeds, gathered from certain volumes of miscellaneous poetry.

Rules for the scholars of the old and classical School of Poetry, which was founded by Homer and Sophocles, and of which Virgil and Horace, Milton, Dryden, and Pope, did not disdain to be disciples, were formerly drawn from a contemplation of the works of the first masters: and it occurred to me that a similar practice might be successfully adopted with respect to the NEW, and (what I presume to denominate) the ANTI-CLASSICAL SCHOOL. Without entering nicely into the minutiæ of criticism, it has been my endeavour to execute this task, under the general heads of subject, ideas, diction, and metre. I cannot flatter myself that this Art of Poetry, if I may so term it, will be honoured with your approbation, but if it fail of receiving that of the Public, I am persuaded that its failure will be attributable to no other cause than the weakness of the execution.

I should be guilty of an insolent and a self-evident falsehood, were I to affect to say that the aim of this little piece is not to hold up your new school to ridicule: but I do truly affirm my belief, that in attempting to excite ridicule, I have employed no unfair exaggeration; that the school is incapable of caricature; and that, if a smile be raised by my illustrations, it will be heightened by a perusal of the originals whence they are drawn. "The force of Nature can no further go;" nor of Art either.

At the same time that I amuse myself, I trust without malignity, at the expence of your Poems, I wish to assure you, that as far as I have any knowledge of your personal characters, I feel for them a high respect. With the friends of humanity and virtue, I venerate your humane feelings and your virtuous principles: with the generality of our countrymen, I acknowledge and admire your talents: but at the same time, with most men of discernment and cultivated minds, I lament the degradation of your genius, and deprecate the propagation of your perverted taste.

I am,

GENTLEMEN,

Your obedient humble servant,

THE AUTHOR.

THE SIMPLICIAD.

P. Should Wyatt spurn whate'er of fair and grand,
Or Grecian grace or Gothic spirit plann'd,
His pow'rs on pasteboard trifles to employ,
The nick-nack semblance of a baby-toy:
Or Flaxman bid the sculptur'd marble wear   5
A vacant simper and a clownish stare;
Who but would laugh the artist's skill to scorn?
Who but his prostituted art would mourn?
And will you then the smile, the sigh refuse,
Daughter of heav'n to see the high-soul'd Muse   10
Condemn'd in leading strings to pipe, and cry,
And lisp the accents of the nursery;

Hor. de Art. Poet.
V. 1. Humano capiti cervicem pictor equinam
Jungere si velit, &c.

Or clad in gipsey rags, with rustic air
To whine with beggars, and with felons swear?

  F. Yet Nature and Simplicity belong——   15

  P. True, to the mighty arbiters of song,
To painters, sculptors, all who claim a part
In the rich heritage of mimic art.
What strikes the soul in that majestic dome,
" The world's just wonder, and ee'n thine, O
    " Rome?"   20
What gives the charm to Raphael's chaste design,
Bids Delphi's God with matchless beauty shine,
And stamps with life " the tale of Troy divine?"

  F. Simplicity.

              P. Yes, not with rags defil'd,
A stamm'ring, stagg'ring, puling, puny child: 25
But the great mother of a noble race,
Full-shap'd, harmonious, firm in voice and pace,
Inform'd by science, and array'd by grace.

  V. 15. ————— pictoribus atque poetis
      Quidlibet audendi semper fuit æqua potestas
      Sed non ut placidis coeant immitia

Most poets err (forgive th' advent'rous strain,
Lords of the lyre, which dares your praise profane)   30
Whilst with a zeal too ardent they pursue
A favourite beauty fondly kept in view.
Rapt with bright Chivalry's romantic song,
Of genius bold, in numbers sweet and strong,
Scott pours the latest Minstrel's lay along;   35
Yet oft, the tale by quaint intrusions crost,
Sense, fancy, feeling shrink from " lost, lost, lost."
Slave of apostrophe, of ah! and oh!
To sober dignity determin'd foe,
Campbell assumes the Andes giant's form,   40
Enthron'd on clouds amid the mountain's storm.
Spirit and ease of each the brave intent,
Burns is familiar, Cowper negligent;
While Virgil smiles to see himself so fine
In graceful Sotheby's embellish'd line,   45
And Camoens mourns, that Strangford sweet and gay
Blurs with unhallow'd spot his modest lay.

V. 29. Maxima pars vatum ———
    Decipimur specie recti.

F. O! if the poet with immodest stain
The heav'nly gift of poesy profane,
In fair array the wanton harlot deck,   50
And wake the blush on Virtue's maiden cheek;
Spare not thy satire's holy rage to pour,
And let its keenest vengeance light on Moore.

P. Less high the purport of my playful rhime,
To sport with folly, not to war with crime;   55
A crime, that manhood shames, and makes the Muse
A go-between and pander to the stews;
A crime, that merits, would that it might draw
On its ripe back the iron scourge of law.

F. Then why assault Simplicity? Her lays   60
Modest and lovely——

           P. Modest! 'tis her praise;
Nor barely modest; Gifford must approve
The friend of mercy, peace, and virtuous love:
(Gifford, the dread of every snivelling fool,
That loves and rhimes by Della Cruscan rule.)   65
And therefore 'tis, Simplicity may claim,
She, or the mongrel that affects her name,

A lighter rod. But for the Muse disgrac'd,
For genius outrag'd, and perverted taste,
The scholar's pity, and the critic's sneer,   70
And smirking ignorance with stare and leer
Attend her triumph : while to greet the song
Enthusiast Folly draws her mimic throng ;
And, as the vapid chorus louder swells,
Her whistle blows, and chimes her coral bells.   75

  O, that thou ever should'st forego thy claim,
Sweet child of Genius, to thy father's fame,
Renounce the glory of thine elder song,
And ape the whimper of a beldame's tongue!
When smiling mild the glorious chief of Troy   80
Unlac'd his helmet, and caress'd his boy ;
Amid the roaring of th' Ægean deep
When Danae cried, " O sleep, my infant, sleep ;"
When her fond spouse o'er Heliodora shed
The tender tear and gave her to the dead,   85
Thine was the song :—thine is the song that wakes
Echo, who sleeps by Albion's northern lakes,
* Echo, whose birth the cuckoo cannot tell,
Tho' that 'tis sound the bird must know full well ;

† Where Poets, dozing in lethargic dream,   90
Such as may Fancy's wayward sons beseem,
Entwine each random weed, that charms their eye,
To hang on wildly-staring Poesy :

AUTHORITIES.

* *Echo, whose birth, &c.* P. 11.
  > Yes! full surely 'twas the Echo,
  >   Solitary, clear, profound,
  > Answering to Thee, shouting Cuckoo!
  >   Giving to thee sound for sound.
  >
  > Whence the voice? from air or earth?
  >   *This the Cuckoo cannot tell;*
  > But a startling sound had birth,
  >   *As the Bird must know full well.*
  >   Poems by W. W. vol. ii. p. 123.

† *Where Poets dozing in lethargic dream, &c.*
  > Then ask not wherefore, here, alone,
  >   Conversing as I may,
  > I sit upon this old gray stone,
  >   And *dream* my time away.
  >   Lyrical Ballads by W. W., I. 3.

  > And as *beseem'd the wayward Fancy's child*
  >   *Entwin'd each random weed that pleas'd mine eye.*
  >   Poems by R. S. Dedicatory Sonnet.

  > Dear native brook! where first young Poesy
  >   *Star'd wildly-eager* in her noontide *dream.*
  >   Poems by S. T. C. p. 39.

* Poets, who fix their visionary sight
On Sparrow's eggs in prospect of delight, 95
† With fervent welcome greet the glow-worm's flame,
Put it to bed and bless it by its name;

AUTHORITIES.

* *Poets, who fix their visionary sight, &c.*
> Look, five blue *eggs* are gleaming there!
> Few *visions* have I seen more fair,
> Nor many *prospects of delight*,
> More pleasing than that simple sight!
> Poems by W. W., II. 53.

† *With fervent welcome greet, &c.*—These lines require some explanation. The Poet tells us that, "Among all lovely things "his Love had been," but had never had the good fortune to see a Glow-worm. Judge of his emotions

> When riding near her home one stormy night
> A single Glow-worm did I chance to espy;
> I gave *a fervent welcome* to the sight,
> And from my horse I leapt; great joy had I.

He then laid the Glow-worm on a leaf, and carried it **away** with him: thereupon what followed, Musa rogata refer:

> When to the dwelling of my Love I came,
>   I went into the orchard quietly;
> And left the Glow-worm, *blessing it by name*,
>   *Laid safely by itself*, beneath a tree.

* Hunt waterfalls, that gallop down the hills :

† And dance with dancing laughing daffodills;

AUTHORITIES.

The whole next day I hoped, and hoped with fear,
At night the Glow-worm shone beneath the tree :
I led my Lucy to the spot, " Look here !"
Oh ! joy it was for her, and joy for me !

Poems by W. W. I. 66.

* *Hunt waterfalls, that gallop down the hills, &c.*

    When up she winds along the brook,
    To *hunt the waterfalls.*   Poems by W. W. I. 8.

    What more he said I cannot tell.
    The stream came thund'ring down the dell,
        And *galloped* loud and fast.

Lyrical Ballads by the same. II. 57.

† *And dance with dancing laughing daffodills, &c.*

    I wander'd lonely as a cloud
    That floats on high o'er vales and hills,
    When all at once I saw a crowd,
    A host of *dancing daffodills.*
    * * * * * *

    A Poet could not be but gay
    In such a *laughing* company.
    * * * * * *

    And then my heart with pleasure fills,
    And *dances with the daffodills.*

Poems by W. W. II. 49.

The whole poem, consisting of eighteen lines, is exquisite.

* Or measure muddy ponds from side to side,   100
And find them three feet long and two feet wide:
Poets † with brother donkey in the dell
Of mild equality who fain would dwell
With ‡ brother lark or brother robin fly,
And flutter with half-brother butterfly;   105

AUTHORITIES.

* *Or measure muddy ponds from side to side, &c.*

> This Thorn you on your left espy,
> And to the left, three yards beyond
> You see a little *muddy pond*
> Of water never dry;
> *I've measur'd it from side to side:*
> *'Tis three feet long, and two feet wide.*
> Lyrical Ballads by W. W. I. 37.

† *With brother donkey in the dell, &c.*—The following lines are taken from an address to a Young Ass, by S. T. C.

> Innocent foal! thou poor despis'd forlorn!
> I hail thee BROTHER, spite of the fool's scorn!
> And fain would take thee with me, *in the Dell*,
> Of peace and *mild equality to dwell.*   p. 53.

‡ *With brother lark or brother robin fly, &c.*

> Up with me! up with me into the clouds!
> For thy song, *Lark*, is strong;

*To woodland shades with liberty repair,
And scorn with pious sneer the House of Pray'r :

> Up with me, up with me into the clouds!
>   Singing, singing,
> With all the heavens about thee ringing,
>   Lift me, guide me, till I find
> The spot which seems so to thy mind!

And so forth, through another page : after which,

> Hearing thee, or else some other,
>   As merry a *brother*, &c.

Poems by W. W. I. 81.

Of the Robin Redbreast, the same Poet singeth sweetly, that he is

> The bird, who by some name or other,
> All men who know him, call him *brother*.

Ibid, p. 16.

The relationship of the Butterfly is not so clearly settled: but in virtue of his being brother to the Robin Redbreast,

> A *brother* he seems of thine own,

I have ventured to give his genealogy as above.

* *To woodland shades, &c.*
  Go thou and seek the House of Prayer!
  I to the woodlands bend my way,
  And meet Religion there!
  She needs not haunt the high-arch'd dome to pray, &c.
  With Liberty she loves to rove.

Poems by R. S. I. 59.

* Of apostolic daisies learn to think,
Draughts from their urns of true devotion drink:

AUTHORITIES.

I transcribe the passage as I find it. It was written, as appears by the date subjoined, in 1795. It is to be hoped that thirteen years have wrought a change in the author's sentiments.

* *Of apostolic daisies learn to think, &c.*—The daisy is a favourite with one of our poets; and with reason: for it is fitting that the flower which is " Nature's favourite," should be also " the Poet's darling." I select one or two passages from " the overflowings of his mind," in praise of that " sweet silent creature."

>Thou breath'st with me in sun and air,
>Do thou, as thou art wont, repair
>My heart with gladness, and a share
> Of thy meek nature!

Again:

>If stately passions in me burn,
>And one chance look to thee should turn,
>I *drink* out of an humbler *urn*
> A lovelier pleasure.

Again:

>At dusk I've seldom mark'd thee press
>The ground, as if in thankfulness,
>Without some feeling more or less,
> *Of true devotion.*

But I know not whether a more perfect instance of silliness is to be detected in the whole farrago of the school, than the

*Woo with fond languishment their chymic maids,
Pray for their † Spaniels; ‡ consecrate their spades;

AUTHORITIES.

following stanza; mark ye! addressed as well as the foregoing, to the daisy:

> Thou wander'st the wide world about,
> Uncheck'd by pride or scrupulous doubt,
> With friends to greet thee, or without,
>   Yet pleased and willing;
> Meek, yielding to occasion's call,
> And all things suffering from all,
> THY FUNCTION APOSTOLICAL
>   IN PEACE FULFILLING.

I may be pardoned for exclaiming with Cowper,

> From such apostles O ye mitred heads
> Preserve the church!

* *Woo with fond languishment their chymic maids, &c.*
  Spirits of Love—
  Or *with fond languishment* around my fair
  Sigh in the loose luxuriance of her hair—
  Spirits! to you the infant maid was given,
  Form'd by the wond'rous *alchemy* of Heaven.
                    Poems by S. T. C. 37.

† *Pray for their spaniels, &c.*—Such a practice is not very common, I apprehend, but we have the Poet's own words for it, that it even was so:

*Whine over tatter'd cloaks and ragged breeches,
And moralize with gatherers of leeches.

AUTHORITIES.

I PRAY'D FOR THEE, and that thy end were past,
And willingly have laid thee here at last.

Poems by W. W. II. 103.

But then " little Music" was not a common dog: it was not for the usual canine qualities that

Both man and woman wept when she was dead.
But for some precious boons vouchsafed to thee
Found scarcely any where in like degree!
For love, that comes to all, the holy sense,
Best gift of God, in thee was most intense;
A chain of heart, a feeling of the mind,
A tender sympathy which did thee bind
Not only to us men, but to thy kind;
Yea for thy fellow-brutes in thee we saw
The soul of Love, Love's intellectual law.

Now if the Poet's partiality for his friend's dog did not obscure his understanding, she certainly was a wonderful creature; and were all such, we might be disposed to adopt the practice of one of our bards and pray for our dogs in this world, and the creed of his friend, with respect to their existence in another.

——Fare thee well! mine is no narrow creed;

Is his valedictory address to a favourite old Spaniel:

——There is another world

For all that live and move—a better one!

Poems by R. S. I. 142.

Surely this is being wise above what is written.

Boast of New Bond-street, and St. Paul's Church-
yard,

With " Lyric Ballads" many a gentle Bard, 115

V. 114. Æmilium circa ludum faber imus et ungues.
Exprimet, et molles imitabitur ære capillos,
Infelix operis summâ.

AUTHORITIES.

‡ *Consecrate their spades, &c.*—From lines to the Spade of a Friend:

And when thou art past service, worn away,
Thee a surviving soul shall *consecrate*.

Poems by W. W. II. 127.

* *Whine over tatter'd cloaks, &c.*—Of the pitiable tales of the tatter'd cloak and the leech-gatherer, I shall have more to say anon. For the circumstance of *the ragged breeches*, I refer to a poem communicated to the Anti-Jacobin Newspaper by a Mr. Higgins: and take this opportunity of recommending to Mr. W. the next time he shall have occasion to request the assistance of a friend, to apply to this gentleman; as I am convinced that the poems of Mr. H. " will in a great measure have
" the same tendency as his own, and that, though there may be
" found a difference, there will be found no discordance in the
" colours of their style; as their opinions on the subject of
" poetry do almost entirely coincide."

See Preface to Lyrical Ballads.

Proud of gilt cover, with engravings grac'd,
Courts of mammas and aunts the curious taste.
'Tis their's with greater than the Doctor's skill,
To make by night the screaming infant still;
Or, welcoming day with some melodious air,   120
Wash his nice hands, and comb his shining hair,
To story told of Gaffer Grumble's wig,
Dame Hubbard's dog, and Betty Pringle's pig.
A simple tale these artless bards rehearse;
The ditty simple, simple is the verse;   125
But ah! in vain—for know a simpler lay
Wrests from their grasp the nursery prize away!

Bards of the lakes! in sickly thoughts sublime,
The vulgar image, and the doggrel rhime,
Less worthy far of go-cart, pap, and bib,   130
Your brethren of the cradle and the crib.
What tho' they dare, when Autumn winds are sobbing,
To chaunt a funeral stave o'er poor Cock Robin,
They * cannot sing how by some name or other,
All men who know him call Cock Robin brother,   135

Then bid old Father Adam ope his eyes,
And shudd'ring see this sight beneath the skies,
How Redbreasts hunt and feed on Butterflies.
What though in simple rhimes to nature true,
They sing of roses red and violets blue,   140

AUTHORITIES.

* *They cannot sing, &c.*—It was some time before I could discover the cause of the appeal made to Father Adam, and referred to above. But after two or three diligent perusals of the poem, the opening of which follows, I perceived it was the indignation of the bard at seeing (eloquar an sileam?) a robin redbreast chasing a butterfly. Fill'd with horror at the spectacle, the poet bursts forth in this animated and pertinent remonstrance:

> Art thou the bird whom man loves best,
> The pious bird with the scarlet breast,
> Our little English Robin;
> The bird that comes about our doors
> When autumn winds are sobbing?
> Art thou the Peter of Norway Boors?
> Their Thomas in Finland,
> And Russia far inland?
> *The bird, whom by some name or other*
> *All men who know thee call their brother,*
> The darling of children and men?
> *Could Father Adam open his eyes,*
> *And see this sight beneath the skies,*
> *He'd wish to close them again.*

Poems by W. W. I. 16.

THE SIMPLICIAD.

Tis not for them to hymn the spring-day praises
Of * patient primroses and † dauntless daisies;

AUTHORITIES.

* *Of patient primroses, &c.*—To the small Celandine:

>Comfort have thou of thy merit
>Kindly, unassuming spirit!
>Careless of thy neighbourhood
>Thou dost show thy pleasant face
>On the moor, and in the wood,
>In the lane—there's not a place,
>Howsoever mean it be,
>But 'tis good enough for thee.
>
>*Ill befal the yellow flowers,*
>Children of the flaring hours!
>*Butter-cups, that will be seen,*
>*Whether we will see or no;*
>*Others too of lofty mien;*
>*They have done as worldlings do,*
>Taken praise that should be thine,
>Little, humble Celandine.

The poet having expressed his admiration of this little flower through seven stanzas of this spirit, and having set it on a footing with the apostolical daisy, by finally saluting it,

>Prophet of delight and mirth,
>Scorned and slighted upon earth,

concludes with declaring his resolution of being more just to its merits,

Indignant show'r in fiddle-faddle verses
Blessings on celandines, on king-cups curses;

AUTHORITIES.

I will sing as doth behove,
Hymns in praise of what I love!

Poems by W. W. I. 26.

The reader perhaps would exclaim, Ohe, jam satis est! Not so the poet, who is not contented without supplying another address of six stanzas in the same gentle strain to the same little flower: Having regretted that he so long could overlook

" Her *arch and wily* ways
And her store of other praise," he continues,

Blithe of heart from week to week
Thou dost play at hide-and-seek,
While *the patient Primrose* sits
Like a Beggar in the cold,
Thou, a Flower of wiser wits,
Slip'st into thy shelter'd hold, &c. p. 29.

‡ — *dauntless daisies, &c.*—The reader is already acquainted with some of the daisy's amiable and Christian virtues; its meekness and humility; its long-suffering and thankfulness; but its resolution and courage are not less worthy of admiration, as the following lines may testify:

In shoals and bands, a morrice train,
Thou greet'st the Traveller in the lane;
If welcome once thou count'st it gain;
Thou art not daunted,
Nor car'st if thou be set at naught——

Poems by W. W. I. 2.

To scold tall flow'rs, which do as worldlings do, 145
And will be seen, whether we'll see or no;
While others blithe of heart from week to week
More arch and wily play at hide-and-seek;
To bless * mysterious cuckoos; and to sing,
With † fancy tether'd to a Linnet's wing, 150

AUTHORITIES.

* *To bless mysterious cuckoos, &c.*——
  O blithe new-comer! I have heard,
  I hear thee and rejoice:
  O cuckoo shall I call thee bird
  Or but a wandering voice?
   *   *   *   *
  Thrice welcome, darling of the spring!
  Even yet thou art to me
  No bird; but an invisible thing,
  A voice, a *mystery*.
   *   *   *   *
  O *blessed* bird, &c. &c.

* *With fancy tether'd to a Linnet's wing, &c.*——
  A whispering leaf is now my joy,
  And then a bird will be the toy,
   That doth my fancy tether.
  Hail to thee, far above the rest,
   In joy of voice and *pinion*
  Thou, *Linnet*, in thy green array.
      Poems by W. W. II. 79.

In numbers shilly-shally, shally-shilly,
So very feeling and so very silly,
That wondering Nonsense proud to see a son
Of Science prate in phrase so like her own,
Dwells on the meagre verse with sparkling eyes, 155
While o'er degraded Genius Reason sighs.

Sad is the triumph of the simple Bard!
Her limbs all fetter'd and her cheeks all marr'd,
Nature her violated kingdom feels,
And sense and judgment blur his chariot wheels. 160
But would ye wish, ye nursery bards, to know
The sources, whence your rivals' glories flow,
Hear, while no brother-mason I impart
The precious mysteries of the sinking art,
And not disposed to dive beneath the flood, 165
Strip off the buoyant cork from those who wou'd.

I. First choose your theme: not one, whose view
Visions of beauty to poetic eyes, [supplies

V. 163. —— fungar vice cotis, acutum
    Reddere quæ ferrum valet, exsors ipsa secandi.

V. 167. Sumite materiam, vestris qui scribitis æquam
    Viribus——.

Charms the rapt soul with scenes of other years,
Or " opes the source of sympathetic tears."   170
Such was the theme, when Southey's feeling song
Invok'd revenge for bleeding Afric's wrong;
And such when Wordsworth bade the Minstrel raise
His festal strain to " Good Lord Clifford's" praise.
For why to distant lands and ages roam?   175
Less hackney'd themes invite you nearer home;
Congenial themes, which yield more tasteful food
* To poets musing in their fitful mood.
See! with impassion'd flow'rs each bank is teeming;
See! with blue sparrow's eggs each hedge is gleaming;   180
†Ecstatic birds, whose thoughts no bard can measure;
Blossoms that breathe, and twigs that pant with pleasure.

AUTHORITIES.

* *To poets musing in their fitful mood.*—" Musings," and " Moods of my own mind" are the titles prefixed by our poets to some of their effusions.

" And madness laughing in his ireful mood", is a noble line from Dryden.

† *Ecstatic birds, whose thoughts no bard can measure;*
Blossoms that breathe, and twigs that pant with pleasure.

Heaths bloom with cups,* the darlings of the eye;
†Green fields with grass, that drinks a sense of joy;

AUTHORITIES.

Upon yon tuft of hazel trees
That twinkle to the gusty breeze,
Behold him perch'd in *ecstasies*.
Poems by W. W. II. 81.

And 'tis my faith that *every flower*
Enjoys the air it breathes.
The *birds* around me hopp'd and play'd;
  Their thoughts I cannot measure:
But the least motion which they made,
  It was a thrill of pleasure.
The budding twigs spread out their fan,
  To catch the breezy air,
And I must think, do all I can,
  That there was pleasure there.
Lyrical Ballads by the same, I. 82.

* *the darlings of the eye, &c.*
  And cups, *the darlings of the eye*,
  So deep is their vermilion die.
Lyrical Ballads, by W. W. I. 37.

† *Green fields with grass that drinks a sense of joy, &c.*
  There is a blessing in the air,
  Which seems *a sense of joy* to yield
  To the bare trees and mountains bare
  And *grass in the green field.*
Ibid. p. 61.

THE SIMPLICIAD.

* Hills have their thorns with clasping mosses hung;   185
Thorns now so old, you'd say they ne'er were young,
Mosses, so close, you'd say that they were bent
With wicked plain and manifest intent,
As if they all had joined in one endeavour,
To kill and bury the poor thorn for ever.   190
The village boasts its busy,† busy bees;
‡Old road-menders who dine on bread and cheese;

AUTHORITIES.

* *Hills have their thorns, with clasping mosses hung, &c.*
  There is a *thorn,—it looks so old,*
  In truth you'd find it hard to say,
  How it could ever have been young
  It looks so old and grey.
  Up from the earth these mosses creep,
  And this poor thorn they clasp *it round*
  So close, you'd say that they were bent
  With plain and manifest intent
  To drag it to the ground;
  And all had joined in one endeavour
  To bury this poor thorn for ever.
  Lyrical Ballads, I. 35, 36.

† *Its busy, busy bees, &c.*   See Poems by R. S. II. 74.
  Thou wert out betimes, thou *busy, busy bee.*
  The appellation is a favourite with the author; it occurs twice four times in four six-line stanzas.

*Poachers, who go, when trade in England fails,
To drink their grog and curse in New South Wales;

AUTHORITIES.

‡ *Old road-menders who dine on bread and cheese, &c.*
> There was an *old man* breaking stones
> To *mend the turnpike way*;
> He sate him down beside a brook,
> And out *his bread and cheese* he took,
> For now it was mid-day.
>
> Poems by R. S. II. 91.

The old turnpike-mender is presently joined by a soldier, with his knapsack on, who enquires "how far to Bristol town;" and having received a full and particular answer, about the road and the foot-path,

> The soldier took his knapsack off
> For he was hot and dry;
> And out *his bread and cheese* he took,
> And he sat down beside the brook
> To *dine* in company.

After such an introduction as this, with what follows about the soldier begging his companion to let him lean his back against the post, for that

> In such a sweltering day as this,
> A knapsack is the devil;

few readers, it is to be presumed, would have much desire to know more.

* *Poachers, who go, &c.*—See Botany Bay Eclogues; by R. S. Poems, Vol. 1. p. 93 and 101.

*Goodies who boil their pottage one and one
By the same fire; and some, who dwell alone;
Beggars, on lies and impudence who thrive,
And cottage girls, who don't know seven from five.
If from such arduous tasks you shrink dismay'd,
Play with your cat, apostrophize your spade :   200
Or †should some donkey cross you on the way,
(Not such as wends with crimson housing gay,

AUTHORITIES.

* *Goodies, who boil their pottage one and one, &c.*
  By the same fire to boil their pottage
   Two poor old dames, as I have known,
  Will often live in one small cottage;
   But she, poor woman! *dwelt alone.*

          Lyrical Ballads, I. 11.

† *Or should some donkey cross you on the way, &c.*—For the four subjects alluded to in the two foregoing couplets, I refer to the Lyrical Ballads and Poems of W. W. This gentleman, who is (I believe) the founder of the simple school, supplies us with the most copious catalogue of illustrations of its merit. But I know not that he has any one composition, so prolific of beauty, as the poem to which allusion is here made: so much so indeed, and written withal in a style so different from the other poems by the same author, of which simplicity is by no means the characteristic, that could I believe him capable of such treachery, I should very strongly suspect that his object

The conscious palfrey of a high-born lass,
But a poor, half-starv'd, plodding, vulgar ass)

AUTHORITIES.

was to quiz his brethren. The allusions above keep so close to the original, that my readers may be spared the trouble of perusing the annexed extract, which however I transcribe for my own justification.

TO A YOUNG ASS,
Its Mother being tethered near it.

Poor little foal of an oppressed race!
I love the languid patience of thy face.
And *oft with gentle hand I give thee bread,*
And clap thy ragged coat, and pat thy head.
But what thy dulled spirit hath dismay'd, &c.?
Do thy *prophetic fears* anticipate
Meek Child of Misery! thy future fate?
The starving meal, and all the thousand aches
Which *patient merit* of the unworthy takes?
Or is thy sad heart thrill'd with *filial pain,*
To see thy wretched Mother's shorten'd chain?
How ASKINGLY *its footsteps* hither bend?
It seems to say, And have I then one friend?
Innocent Foal! thou poor despis'd forlorn!
I HAIL THEE BROTHER—SPITE OF THE FOOL'S SCORN!
And fain would take thee with me, &c.
Yea! and more *musically sweet* to me
Thy dissonant *harsh bray* of joy would be
Than warbled melodies, &c.

Poems by S. T. C. p. 52.

'Tis but with gentle hand to give him bread, 205
And clap his ragged coat, and pat his head,
Lament his sad prophetic fears, approve
His patient merit, and his filial love,
Converse a little with his asking feet,
And praise his hoarse bray, musically sweet; 210
Then in despite of scornful folly's pother,
Ask him to live with you, and hail him Brother!

Such subjects are original, 'tis true;
But then they're very poor and paltry too.
And thro' the frame so swiftly venom speeds, 215
So hard it is to purge a field from weeds,
'Tis chance but themes like these infect your style,
Debase your thoughts, and make your language vile.

Not but the bard can wave his wizard wand,
And turn a desert into fairy land, 220
Of village spoils a manly trophy raise,*
And crown a Sofa with a Georgic's praise,

V. 217. —— cui lecta potenter erit res,
Nec facundia deseret hunc, nec lucidus ordo.
Verbaque provisam rem non invita sequentur.

---

* See the Poems of the Rev. George Crabbe, especially The Village and The Parish Register.

II. But like your models, bolder ye defy
Selection, combination, energy.
As in review your throng'd ideas pass,   225
Survey'd in memory's reflective glass,
To every rule of sober reason blind,
Cull out the worst, and leave the best behind.
Or if some nobler thought will venture forth,
As tho' we slight we cannot stifle worth,   230
So marr'd and mangled let it court the view,
Rang'd cheek by jowl beside the antic crew,
And so disfigur'd and disguis'd withal
In babyish style and phrase fantastical,
That the nice eye may sickening turn away   235
From such mean fellowship and coarse array,
While *Fun salutes the charmer Folly bride,
And Laughter tickles Humour's shaking side.

V. 223. Ordinis hæc virtus erit et verus, aut ego fallor.

AUTHORITIES.

* *While Fun salutes the charmer Folly bride, &c.*
Where toil shall call the charmer Health his bride,
And Laughter tickle Plenty's ribless side.

Ibid. p. 53.

III. For be your thoughts attir'd like Falstaff's pack,
Poor hungry knaves with lean and shirtless back. 240
*What that attire is, dost thou ask of me?
Come walk abroad, and I will answer thee.
Yon children, 'mid the strawberries at play;
Yon old man breaking stones on the highway;
Yon lieing gipsey with her sea of tears;
Yon convict wretch that laughs and prays and swears;
Only ask them, as thou hast ask'd of me,
What words to use and they will answer thee!

V. 239. In verbis etiam tenuis cautɞsque serendis,
  Hoc amet, hoc spernat promissi carminis auctor.

AUTHORITIES.

* *What that attire is, dost thou ask of me? &c.*—For the striking form in which this precept is conveyed, I am indebted to a poem by R. S. intituled, The Complaints of the Poor. It opens in the following beautifully abrupt manner.

  And wherefore do the poor complain?
   The rich man ask'd of me;—
  Come walk abroad with me, I said,
   And I will answer thee.

Having met and conversed with several poor objects, miserable enough, Heaven knows, but over whose miseries the poet

But tho' you deem the style of art *too good
And bright for simple Nature's constant food, 250
Yet spurn not what belike may help along
†Your lagging skeletons of meagre song,

V. 249. Dixeris egregiè notum si callida verbum
Reddiderit junctura novum. Si forte necesse est
Indiciis monstrare recentibus abdita rerum, &c.
Et nova fictaque nuper habebunt verba fidem.

AUTHORITIES.

has contrived to throw a strong shade of the ludicrous, they settle the question thus:

> I turn'd me to the rich man then,
> For silently stood he,——
> *You ask'd me why the poor complain,*
> *And these have answer'd thee!*   II. 70.

* *Too good and bright for simple Nature's constant food, &c.*—The two following lines are from a poem, to which there is no title, and which I have read again and again, but am unable to say what is the subject of it. It begins, She was a phantom of delight, and after going on to say that she was an apparition, a shape, an image, a spirit, and a woman, it calls her

> A creature not *too bright or good*
> *For human nature's daily food;*

whatever it was, it appears to have been too much for the Poet's senses.

† *Your lagging skeletons of meagre song, &c.*
> I never saw aught like to them,

As *budding groves wak'd by the vernal tune,
Bestir themselves to spur the steps of June.
For †visitings of thought beyond the reach, 255
The scope, the eye-mark of our English speech,
Behold your mighty master ‡FURIUS brings
New words to temper your sweet jargonings;

AUTHORITIES.

Unless perchance it were
The skeletons of leaves that *lag*
My forest brook along.

Ballads, I. 83.

* *As budding groves wak'd by the vernal tune, &c.*
——————the voice
Of waters which the winter had supplied,
Was soften'd down into a *vernal tone.*
The budding groves appear'd as if in haste,
To spur the steps of June.

Ballads, II. 177.

† *For visitings of thought beyond the reach, &c.*
With no restraint but such as springs
From quick and eager *visitings*
Of thoughts, that lie beyond the reach,
Of thy few words *of English speech.*

Poems by the same, II. 26.

Or bids the old in awkward union close,

*A hailstone swarm ; his godlike task foregoes 260

Of spitting snow on hoary Alpine rocks,

To †steep in silence British weathercocks.

He wills ; the ‡rivers trample to the deep,

The §cataracts blow their trumpets from the steep,

AUTHORITIES.

† *Behold your mighty master Furius brings, &c.*
    Sometimes all little birds that are,
    How they seemed to fill the sea and air
    With their *sweet jargoning !*

Ballads, I. 170.

My reader needs hardly to be reminded that Furius was a Roman poet of genius, but known to us not very favourably by a specimen of his style preserved by Horace and Quinctilian, and imitated above in the 261st verse. Furius hybernas canâ nive conspuit alpes.

* *A hailstone swarm, &c.*
    When *hailstones* have been falling *swarm on swarm.*

Poems by W. W. II. 49.

† *To steep in silence British weathercocks, &c.*
    The moonlight *steeped in silentness*
    The steady *weathercock.*

Ballads, I. 179.

‡ *The rivers trample to the deep, &c.*
    The lightning, the fierce wind, and *trampling* waves.

Poems by W. W. II. 144.

Awaken'd echoes through the mountains throng, 265
And *kettles whisper their faint undersong.

IV. With loftiest numbers, uncontrol'd by rhime,
In epic glory Milton stands sublime;
Such Thomson chose, and Cowper, to array
In moral beauty the descriptive lay. 270
The finished couplet Pope's smooth rhimes approve,
For precept terse, or tender tale of love.

V. 267. Res gestæ regumque ducumque, et tristia bella
Quo scribi possent numero, monstrarit Homerus, &c.

AUTHORITIES.

§ *The cataracts blow their trumpets from the steep, &c.* p. 38.
  The cataracts blow their trumpets from the steep,
  No more shall grief of mine the season wrong,
  I hear *the echoes through the mountains throng,*
  The winds come to me from the fields of sleep.

Ibid, 148.

* *And kettles whisper their faint undersong, &c.*
  To sit without emotion, hope, or aim,
  By my half-kitchen my half-parlour fire,
  And listen to the flapping of the flame,
  Or kettle whispering its faint undersong.

Ibid. 119.

While Nature owns the elegiac strains,
In solemn quatrain pensive Gray complains,
Or strikes to loftier verse the varying lyre, 275
Divides the crown, and rivals Dryden's fire.
But * ye for metre rummage Percy's Reliques;
In sapphics limp, or amble in dactylics;
Trip it in Ambrose Philips's trochaics;
In dithyrambics vault; or hobble in prosaics. 280
Yours† be the linnet's note, teem'd forth in gushes;
And yours the drunken lark's, as up he rushes;

V. 277. Descriptas servare vices operumque colores
Cur ego, si nequeo ignoroque, poeta salutor.

AUTHORITIES.

* *But ye for metre, &c.*—See Lyrical Ballads, and Poems by W. W. and Poems by R. S. passim. " Dithyrambic, a song in honour of Bacchus, in which anciently, and now among the Italians, the distraction of ebriety is imitated." *(See Johnson's Dictionary.)* I know no term equally fit to describe that undefinable measure which spurns all rules and betrays a total alienation of mind, as in Vol. I. p. 80, and Vol. II. p. 147, of Poems by W.W. In the former place the reader will find " *The drunken lark.*"

† *Your's be the linnet's note, teem'd forth in gushes, &c.*
 While thus before my eyes he gleams,
 A brother of the leaves he seems,

*And yours the fiery nightingale's, that sings
With skirmish and capricious passagings.
Why fetter Genius? But as e'er you hope   285
To shun the praise of Dryden and of Pope,
The graceful ease, the stately march decline,
And manly vigour of a classic line.

Thus subject, image, language, metre cull,
Spite of resisting genius, you'll be dull: 290

V. 289. Non satis est pulchra esse poemata, dulcia sunto,
   Et quocunque volent, animum auditoris agunto.
   ————————— male si mandata loqueris,
   Aut dormitabo aut ridebo.

AUTHORITIES.

  When in a moment forth he *teems*,
   His little song in gushes.   Ibid. 81.

* *And yours the fiery nightingale's, &c.*
  O *nightingale*, thou surely art,
  A creature of a *fiery* heart.
        Poems by W. W. I. 42.

  They answer and provoke each other's songs,
 With skirmish and capricious passagings.
        Ballads, I. 93.

But to th' abyss of bathos would you creep,
Unfailing source of ridicule or sleep,
For themes of sorrow marshal all your art,
And plant your whole artillery at the heart.

* Now the gruff farmer's dozing conscience wake,
With tale of Harry Gill and Goody Blake.
Poor Goody Blake, and cruel Harry Gill!
She stole his hedges, and he used her ill,
And now his teeth they chatter, chatter, still.
Now rouse maternal fears for Betty Foy,*   300
Her lamblike pony, and her idiot boy;

AUTHORITIES.

* *Now the gruff farmer's dozing conscience wake, &c.*—See Goody Blake and Harry Gill, a True Story, by W. W. which begins thus:

> O what's the matter, what's the matter?
> What is't that ails young Harry Gill?
> That evermore *his teeth they chatter,*
> *Chatter, chatter, chatter, still.*

Ballads, I. 9.

† *Betty Foy.*—Her history, whether true or not does not appear, occupies thirty pages of the same volume. Johnny's answer to his mother's question where he had been all night,

Who went to fetch the Doctor, but he staid
Beside the water, while the pony fed,
Took the pale moon-beam for the sun, nor knew
The cock's shrill clarion from the owl's to-whoo! 305
Let Pity now the *one-eyed huntsman wail,
Whose legs are wither'd, and whose ancles swell,

AUTHORITIES.

what he had heard, and what he had seen, is contained in the following lines, which may serve as a sample for their four hundred and fifty brethren:

>And thus to Betty's question, he
>Made answer like a traveller bold,
>(His very words I give to you)
>" *The cocks did crow to-whoo, to-whoo,*
>*And the sun did shine so cold.*"
>—Thus answer'd Johnny in his glory,
>And that was all his travel's story.   p. 129.

* *The one-eyed huntsman wail, &c.*
>A long *blue* livery *coat* has he
>That's fair behind and fair before;
>Full five-and-twenty years he lived
>A running huntsman merry;
>And though he has but *one eye* left,
>*His cheek is like a cherry.*
>And he is lean, and he is sick,
>His dwindled body's half awry;

Plumb-coated, cherry-cheek'd Old Simon Lee!
Or the blind † Highland Boy who went to sea,

AUTHORITIES.

His ancles they are swoln and thick,
His legs are thin and dry.

And again;

—Still the more he works, the more
His poor old ancles swell. Ibid. p. 84.

* *Or the blind Highland Boy who went to sea, &c.*
A Highland Boy! why call him so?
Because, my darlings, ye must know,
In land where many a mountain towers,
Far higher hills than these of ours!
He from his life had liv'd.

This Blind Boy, it seems, lived near a lake, and having heard strange tales of mariners, conceived an invincible desire for going to sea, which he at length took an opportunity of effecting in such a vessel, as " ne'er before, did human creature leave the shore."

But say, what was it? Thought of fear!
Well may ye tremble when ye hear!
A HOUSEHOLD TUB, LIKE ONE OF THOSE,
WHICH WOMEN USE TO WASH THEIR CLOTHES,
This carried the Blind Boy.
Poems by W. W. II. 66.

High land 'tis called, because it is not low,
And land because it is not sea, I trow;
He went, and how? in Household Tub, like those
Which washer-women use to wash their clothes.

  Now " shrill your dolours forth" for *Alice Fell,
The little girl in Durham, who doth dwell;   315
Wretch! as behind a bard's post-chaise she rode,
Loose in the wind her tatter'd garment flow'd:
She saw it not, till in the wheel entangled
Like any garden scare-crow there it dangled.
But in the chaise, the child, good man! he took 320
Drove to the inn, and of the host bespoke
For her of duffil grey another cloak.

AUTHORITIES.

  * *Alice Fell, &c.*—For the detail of the poor orphan's disaster, I refer to Poems by W. W. II. 87. Her comfort and subsequent exultation thus sweetly conclude the narrative:

> *Up to the tavern-door we post;*
> Of Alice and her grief I told;
> And *I gave money to the host,*
> *To buy a new cloak for the old.*
> " *And let it be of* DUFFIL GREY,
> As warm a cloak as man can sell.

Let deeper tones the grey-hair'd man deplore,
The old * leech-gatherer on the lonely moor!
See! motionless he stands, and like a cloud, 325
That heareth not the winds which call so loud,
And now upon the water he doth look;
And readeth there as if he read his book;
And stirreth now the pond about his feet,
And tho' with not a leech he there can meet, 330
He smiles so sweetly on his state forlorn,
That gazing bards may laugh themselves to scorn.

AUTHORITIES.

Proud creature was she the next day,
The little orphan, Alice Fell!

* *The old leech-gatherer, &c.*

I saw a man before me unawares,
The oldest man he seem'd, that ever wore grey hairs.

* * *

Motionless as a cloud the old man stood,
That heareth not the loud winds when they call,
And moveth altogether, if it move at all.
At length himself unsettling, he the pond
Stirred with his staff, and fixedly did look

And then bid horror harrow up the soul
With grannam's * tale of blear-eyed collier Moll!

AUTHORITIES.

*Upon the muddy water, which he conn'd
As if he had been reading in a book.*

* * *

He with a *smile* did then his words repeat;
And said that *gathering leeches*, far and wide
He travelled, *stirring thus about his feet*
The waters of the pond where they abide.
Once I could meet with them on every side,
But they have dwindled long by slow decay;
Yet still I persevere, and find them where I may.

* * *

————when he ended,
I could have laughed myself to scorn, to find
In that decrepit man so firm a mind.
" God, said I, be my help and stay secure;
I'll think of the leech-gatherer on the lonely moor."
Poems by W. W. I. 97.

I here take my leave of this author, with an apology for attempting to give any thing like a fair specimen of the solemn buffoonery of this last poem, by my abstract and garbled quotations.

* *With grannam's tale of blear-eyed collier Moll.*—See the Grandmother's Tale, an English eclogue, by R. S. (Poems

Ah! what avail'd her limbs for labour form'd, 335
The coals she carried, and the dogs she worm'd,
Her heart that kindly for her asses felt,
And tongue that curses like a trooper dealt?

AUTHORITIES.

vol. ii. p. 186.) unrivalled for naked vulgarity. Not a syllable of it, any more than the last-mentioned, can be omitted, without injuring the effect of the whole. I must be contented however to copy (and loathsome enough the task is) such passages as are necessary to justify the allusions. Unsupported by the original, they might reasonably enough be scouted for caricatures.

> She used to weed in the garden here, and *worm*
> *Your uncle's dogs, and serve the house with coal.*
> ——————for *poor Moll*
> Was always welcome.
>
> HARRY.
> O 'twas BLEAR-EYED MOLL
> *The* COLLIER *woman,* a great ugly woman,
> I've heard of her.
>
> GRANDMOTHER.
> Ugly enough, poor soul!
> At ten yards distance you could hardly tell
> If it were man or woman, for her voice
> Was rough as our old *mastiff*'s, and she wore
> A man's old coat and hat,—and then her face!

What, that her husband once she left in bed,
(Her flannel night-cap muffled up his head)   340
Put on his breeches, and with mastiff face
Went to the press-gang captain in his place?
One morn they found her in the stable dead,
Kill'd by a cruel smuggler, and her head
Hung (for her throat was cut from ear to ear)   345
Just by a bit of skin, oh dear! oh dear!—

AUTHORITIES.

There was a merry story told of her,
How when the press-gang came to take her husband
As they were both in bed, she heard them coming,
Drest John up in her night-cap, and *herself*
Put on his clothes and went before the Captain.
      *   *   *   *   *

———And *she lov'd her beasts. For tho' poor wretch*
She was a terrible reprobate and swore
Like any trooper, she was always good
To the dumb creatures———
There was a fellow who had oftentimes
Ill-used her asses. He was one who lived
By *smuggling,* and, for she had often met him
Crossing the down at night, she threaten'd him,
If he tormented them again, to inform

Now shame to genius, learning, feeling, sense!
Poets of old to Nature made pretence,
Yet did they not for naked Nature scorn
Art that refines, and graces that adorn, 350
The fancy bright, the eloquence divine,
And soul that lives along the breathing line.
But when this itch for simpleness can blind
The sight, and quell the vigour of the mind,

V. 348. Graiis ingenium, Graiis dedit ore rotundo
         Musa loqui.
V. 353. ——An hæc animos ærugo——
    Cum semel imbuerit, speramus carmina fingi
    Posse linenda cedro, et lævi servanda cupresso?
    Hic meret æra liber Sosiis; hic & mare transit,
    Et longum noto scriptori prorogat ævum.

AUTHORITIES.

Of his unlawful ways. Well, so it was—
'Twas what they both were born to; he provoked her,
She laid an information, and *one morning*
They found her in the stable, her throat cut
From ear to ear, 'till the head only hung
Just by a bit of skin.
                JANE.
            OH DEAR! OH DEAR!

Shades of the Sosii! can we fondly hope 355
To draw admiring crowds to Longman's shop,
Bound in gilt calf thro' Britain's shires to speed,
And bring home laurels from beyond the Tweed?
Saw ye not late the critics lash addrest—

F. All idle prattle—critics may protest 360
Gainst babyish simpleness in nonsense drest,
But novelty will gain a brief applause;
And spite of reason's and the critic's laws,
Loungers and girls will read as fashion draws.

P. But for the Bard—

F. Why he must have his way: 365
Who will not see it, may exclude the day.
And when the fit's on, 'tis as well to kill,
As strive to cure a madman 'gainst his will.

V. 365. ———sit jus liceatque perire poetis;
Invitum qui servat, idem facit occidenti.

THE END.

T. Gillet, Printer, Crown-court.